[redacted]

GRAPHIC LIBRARY™

DISASTERS IN HISTORY

THE GREAT CHICAGO FIRE OF 1871

by Kay Melchisedech Olson

illustrated by Phil Miller and
Charles Barnett III

Consultant:

Richard F. Bales, author

*The Great Chicago Fire and the
Myth of Mrs. O'Leary's Cow*

Capstone

Mankato, Minnesota

Graphic Library is published by Capstone Press,
151 Good Counsel Drive, P.O. Box 669, Mankato, Minnesota 56002.
www.capstonepress.com

Printed in the United States of America

1 2 3 4 5 6 11 10 09 08 07 06

Library of Congress Cataloging-in-Publication Data
Olson, Kay Melchisedech.
The Great Chicago Fire of 1871 / by Kay M. Olson; illustrated by Phil Miller and Charles Barnett III.
p. cm.—(Graphic library. Disasters in history)
Includes bibliographical references and index.
ISBN-13: 978-0-7368-5480-1 (hardcover)
ISBN-10: 0-7368-5480-0 (hardcover)
ISBN-13: 978-0-7368-6875-4 (softcover pbk.)
ISBN-10: 0-7368-6875-5 (softcover pbk.)
1. Great Fire, Chicago, Ill., 1871—Juvenile literature. 2. Fires—Illinois—Chicago—History—19th century—Juvenile literature. 3. Chicago (Ill.)—History—To 1875—Juvenile literature. I. Miller, Phil, ill. II. Barnett, Charles, III, ill. III. Title. IV. Series.
F548.42.O47 2006
977.3'11041—dc22 2005029861

Summmary: In graphic novel format, tells the story of the Great Chicago Fire of 1871, an inferno that forever changed the city's skyline.

Art Direction and Design
Bob Lentz

Storyboard and Production Artist
Alison Thiele

Colorist
Matt Webb

Editor
Donald Lemke

TABLE of CONTENTS

CHAPTER 1
FIRST FLAMES

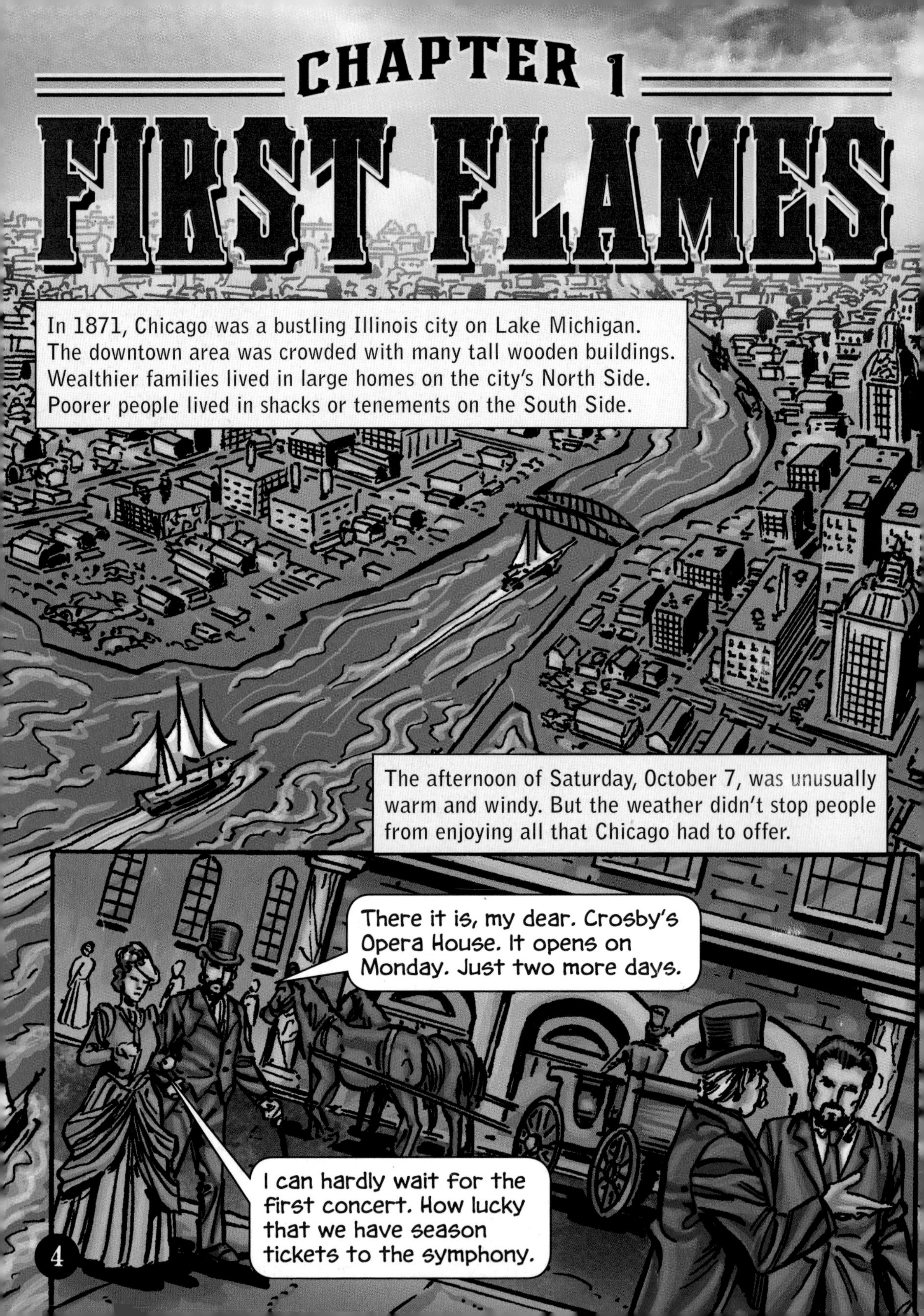
In 1871, Chicago was a bustling Illinois city on Lake Michigan. The downtown area was crowded with many tall wooden buildings. Wealthier families lived in large homes on the city's North Side. Poorer people lived in shacks or tenements on the South Side.
The afternoon of Saturday, October 7, was unusually warm and windy. But the weather didn't stop people from enjoying all that Chicago had to offer.
There it is, my dear. Crosby's Opera House. It opens on Monday. Just two more days.
I can hardly wait for the first concert. How lucky that we have season tickets to the symphony.

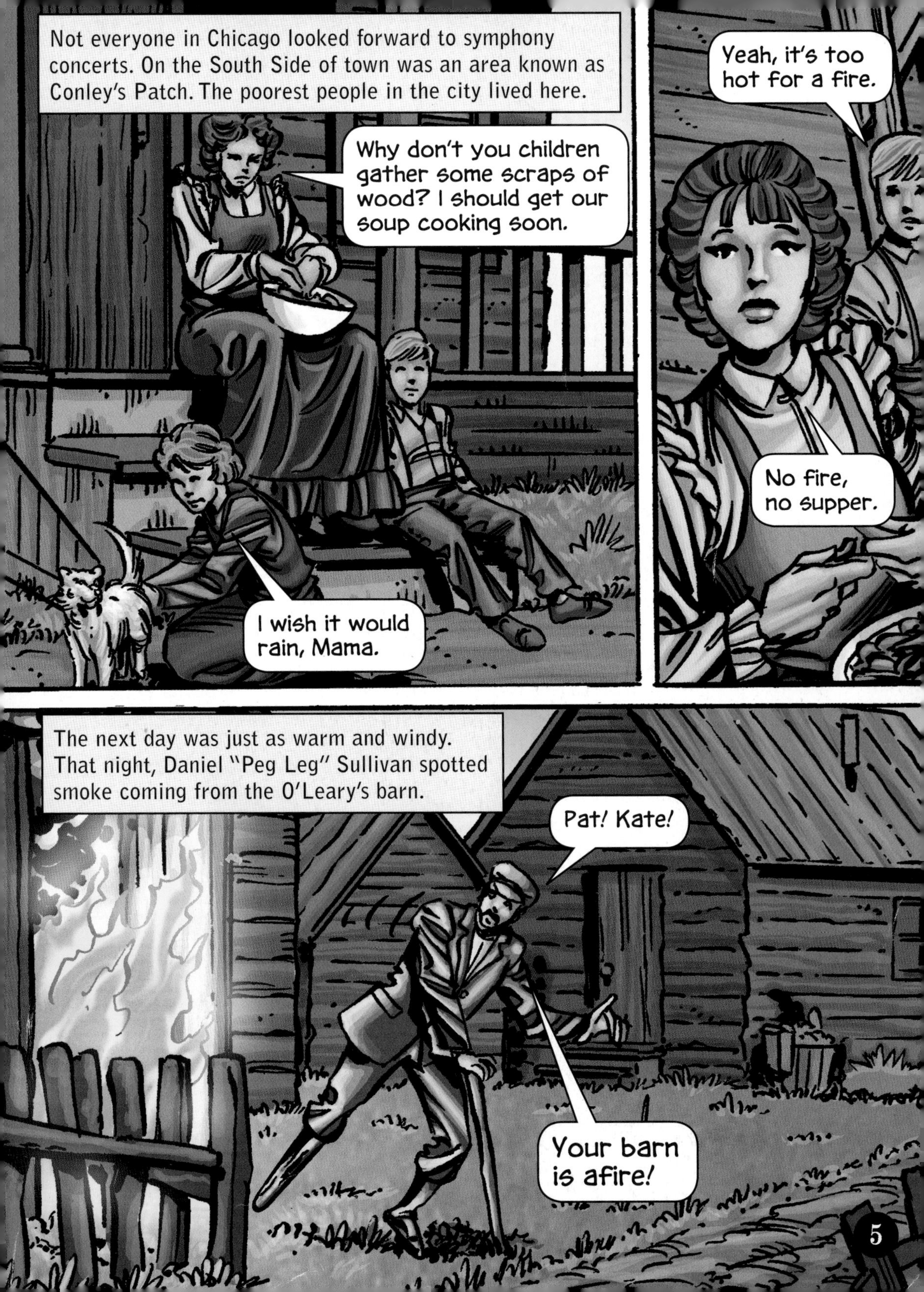

Not everyone in Chicago looked forward to symphony concerts. On the South Side of town was an area known as Conley's Patch. The poorest people in the city lived here.
Why don't you children gather some scraps of wood? I should get our soup cooking soon.
I wish it would rain, Mama.
Yeah, it's too hot for a fire.
No fire, no supper.
The next day was just as warm and windy. That night, Daniel "Peg Leg" Sullivan spotted smoke coming from the O'Leary's barn.
Pat! Kate!
Your barn is afire!

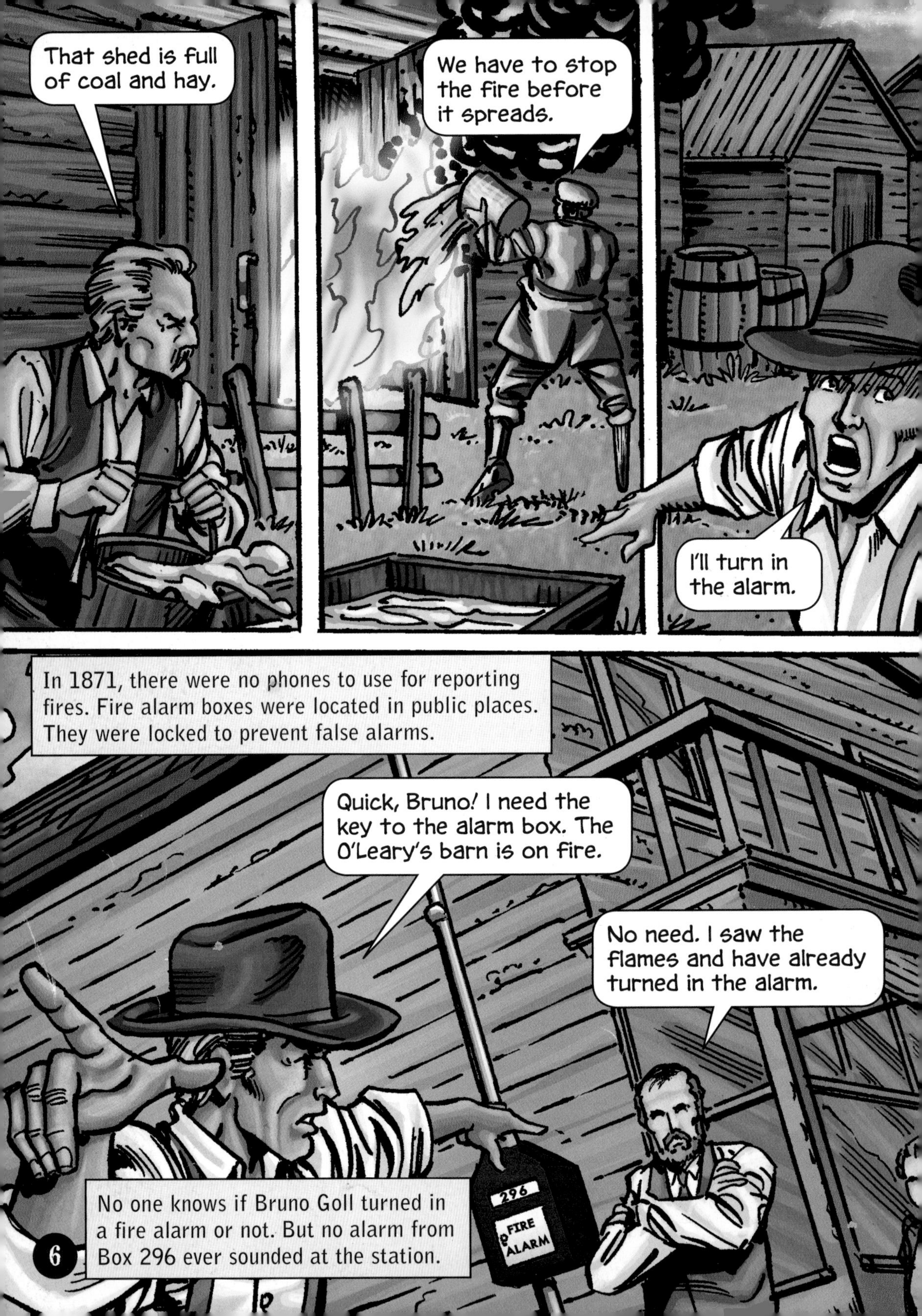
That shed is full of coal and hay.
We have to stop the fire before it spreads.
I'll turn in the alarm.
In 1871, there were no phones to use for reporting fires. Fire alarm boxes were located in public places. They were locked to prevent false alarms.
Quick, Bruno! I need the key to the alarm box. The O'Leary's barn is on fire.
No need. I saw the flames and have already turned in the alarm.
296
FIRE ALARM
No one knows if Bruno Goll turned in a fire alarm or not. But no alarm from Box 296 ever sounded at the station.

7

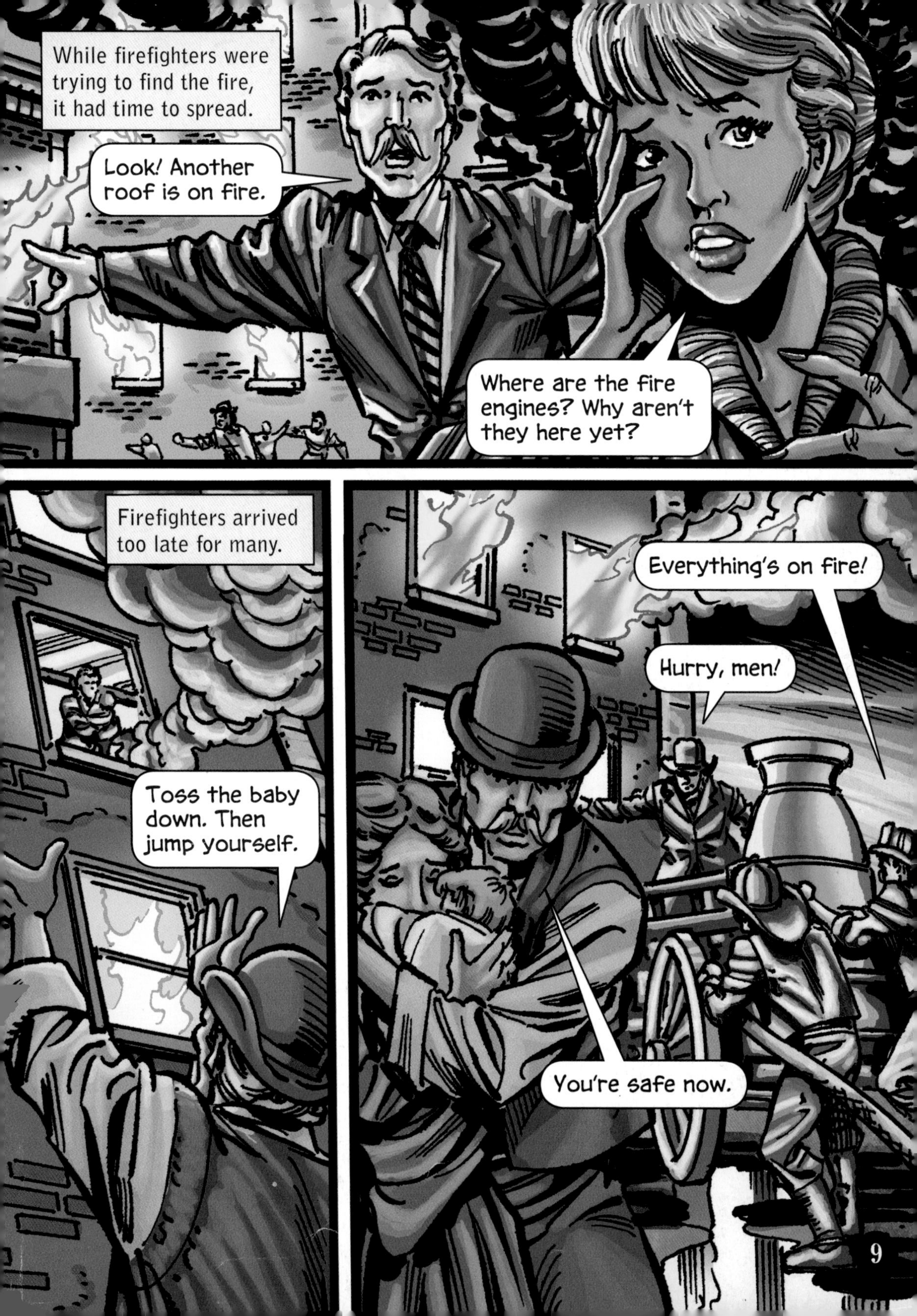
While firefighters were trying to find the fire, it had time to spread.
Look! Another roof is on fire.
Where are the fire engines? Why aren't they here yet?
Firefighters arrived too late for many.
Toss the baby down. Then jump yourself.
Everything's on fire!
Hurry, men!
You're safe now.

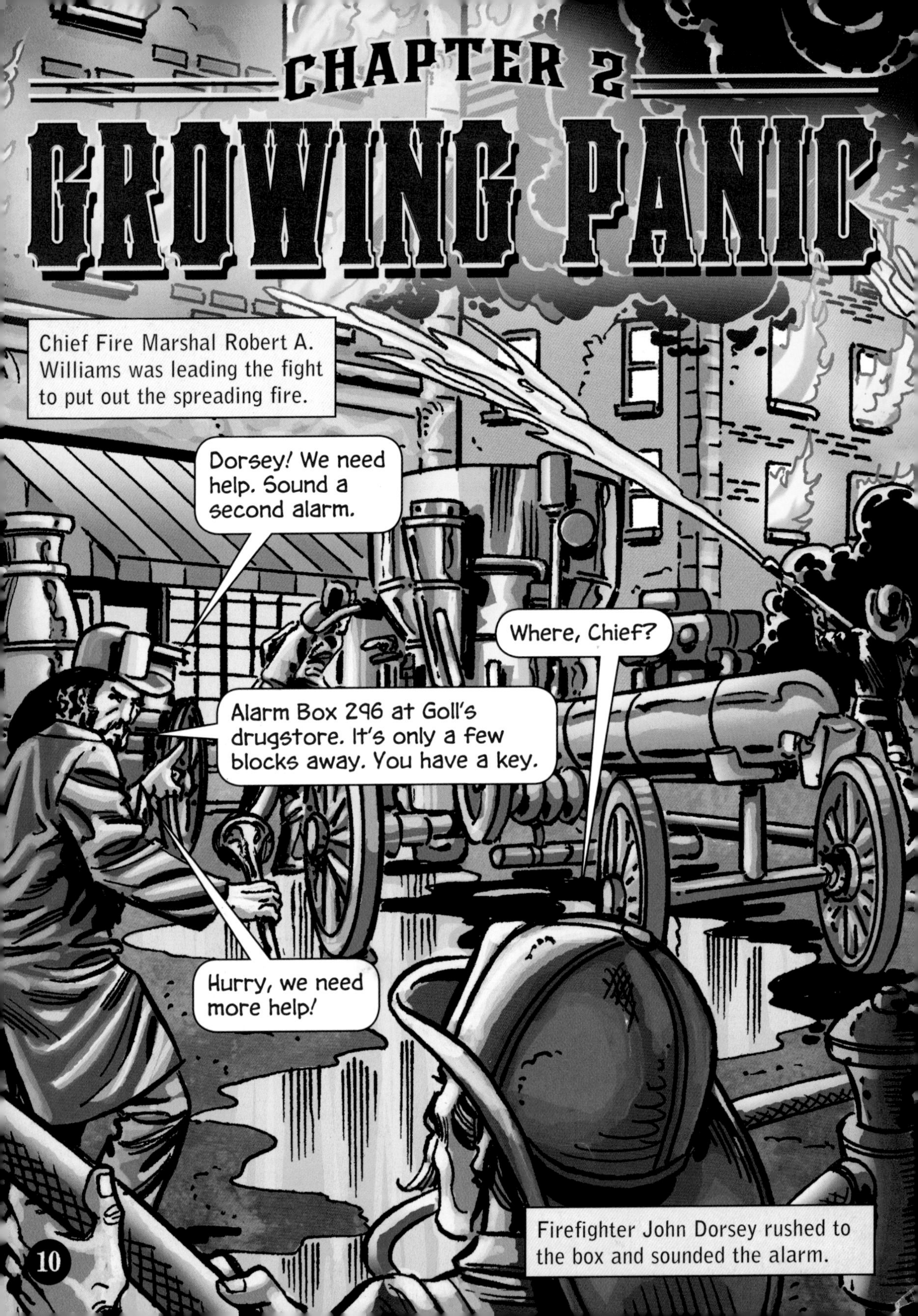
CHAPTER 2
GROWING PANIC
Chief Fire Marshal Robert A. Williams was leading the fight to put out the spreading fire.
Dorsey! We need help. Sound a second alarm.
Where, Chief?
Alarm Box 296 at Goll's drugstore. It's only a few blocks away. You have a key.
Hurry, we need more help!
Firefighter John Dorsey rushed to the box and sounded the alarm.

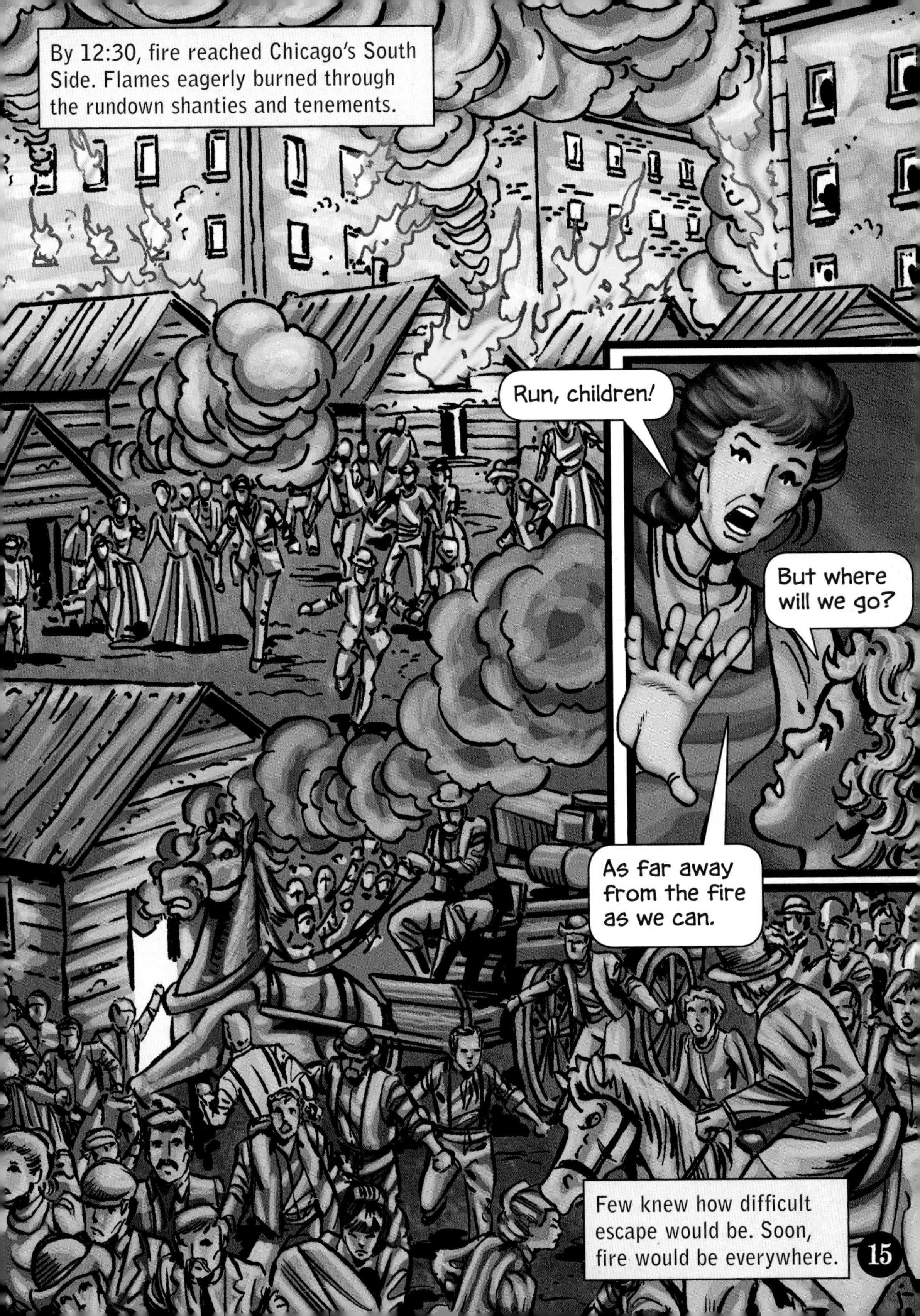
By 12:30, fire reached Chicago's South Side. Flames eagerly burned through the rundown shanties and tenements.
Run, children!
But where will we go?
As far away from the fire as we can.
Few knew how difficult escape would be. Soon, fire would be everywhere.

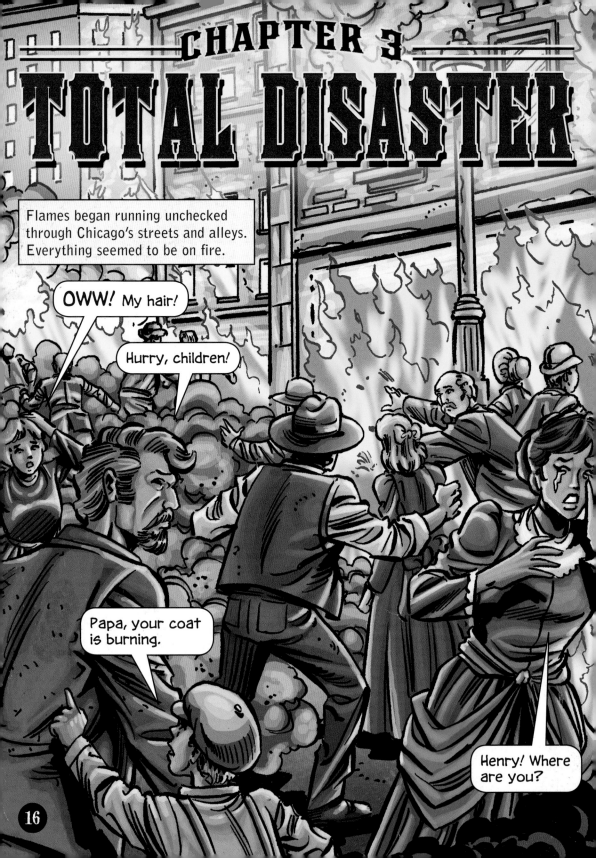

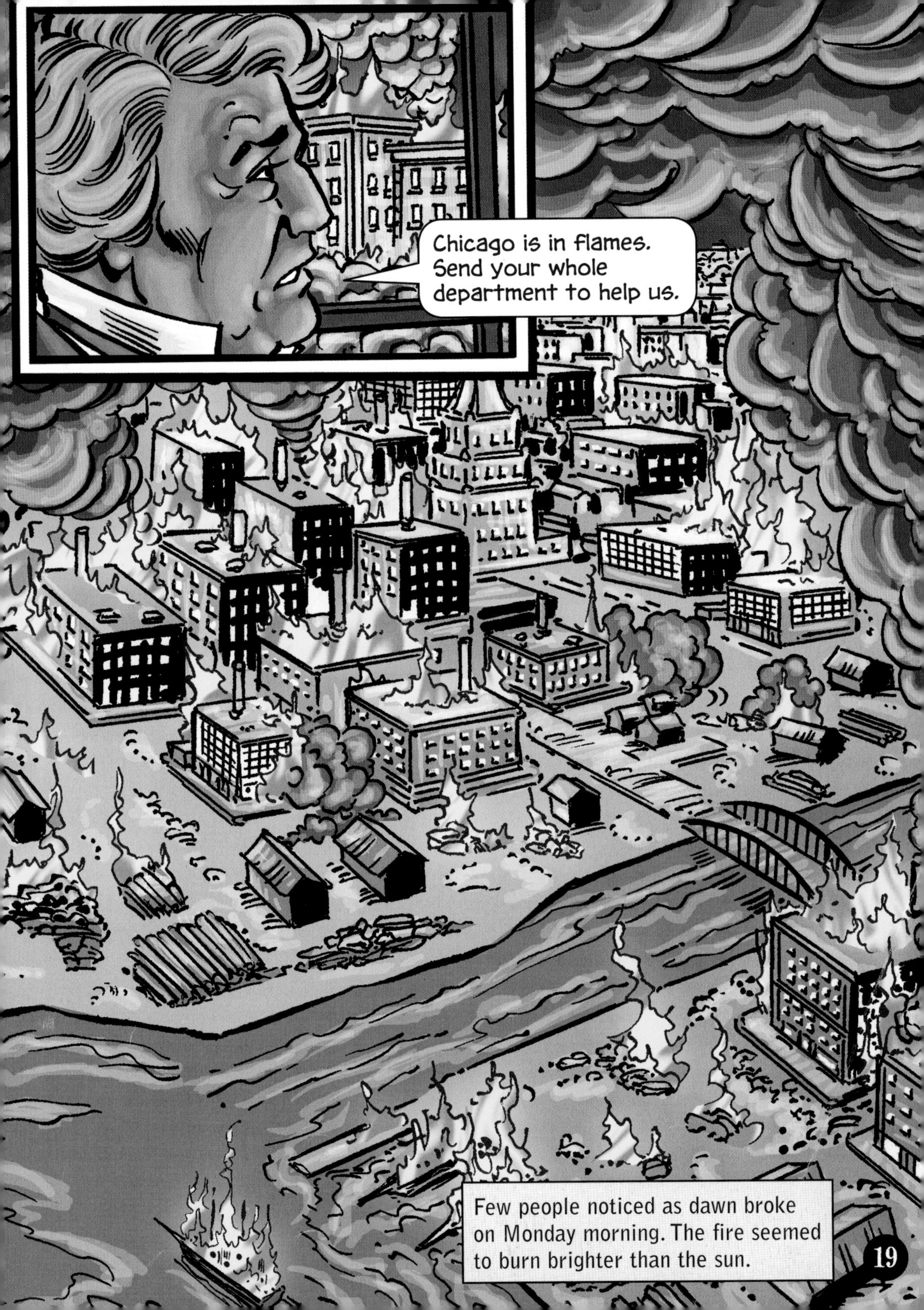
Chicago is in flames. Send your whole department to help us.
Few people noticed as dawn broke on Monday morning. The fire seemed to burn brighter than the sun.

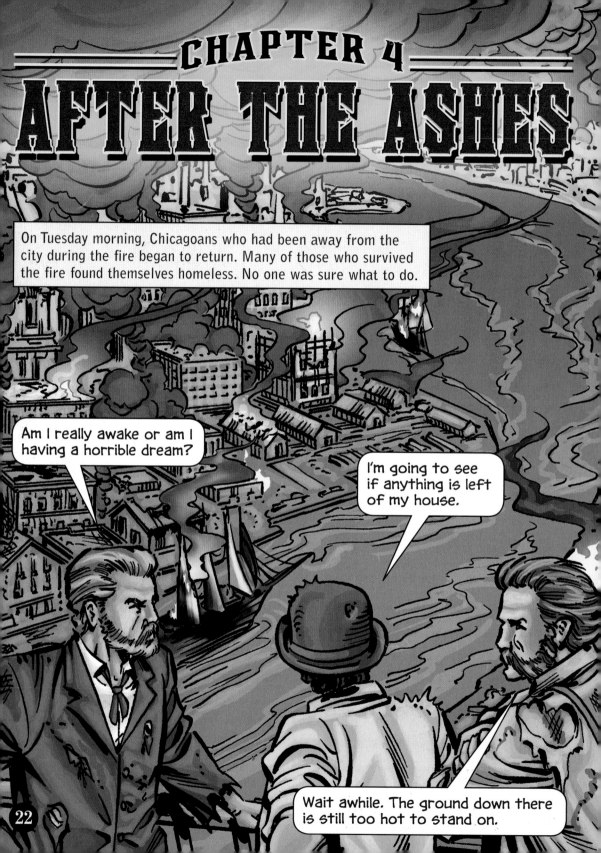

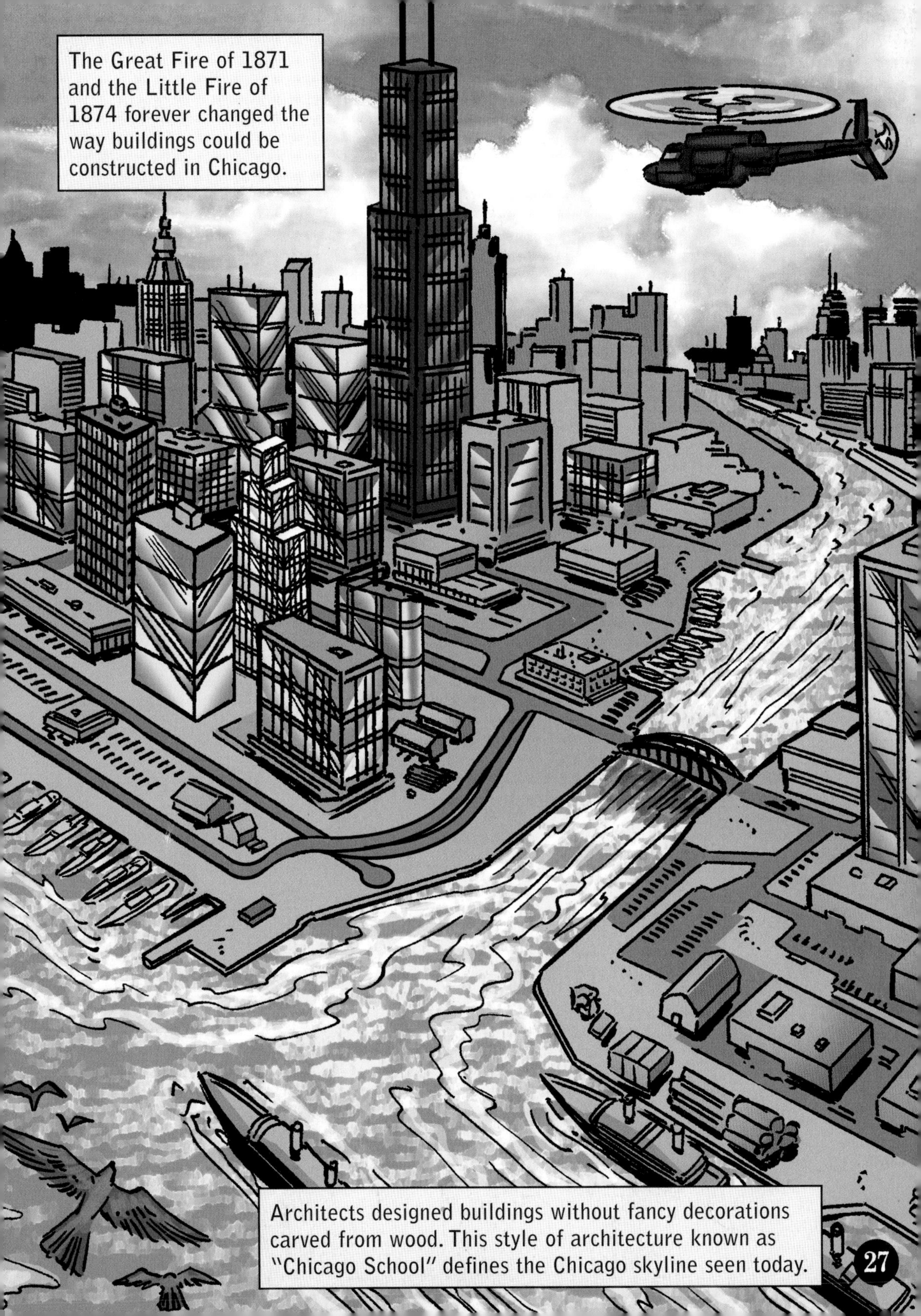
The Great Fire of 1871 and the Little Fire of 1874 forever changed the way buildings could be constructed in Chicago.
Architects designed buildings without fancy decorations carved from wood. This style of architecture known as "Chicago School" defines the Chicago skyline seen today.

MORE ABOUT THE CHICAGO FIRE

At the time of the Great Fire, Chicago was the fourth largest city in the United States. About 334,000 people lived in the city. The Great Fire killed about 300 people and left another 100,000 homeless. The Great Fire destroyed property valued at $192,000,000.

In 1871, telephones, radios, and televisions did not exist. Most people in Chicago did not know about the fire until they saw the flames or neighbors knocked on their doors. Telegraph messages sent word of Chicago's fire to other cities. Fire engines from nearby towns could not arrive in time to help fight the fire.

How did the Great Fire start? No one is sure, but we do know it started in the O'Leary barn. Many myths and legends suggest Catherine O'Leary's cow kicked over a lantern that started the fire. But Patrick and Catherine O'Leary were in bed when the fire started. Many people unfairly accused the O'Learys of causing Chicago's Great Fire.

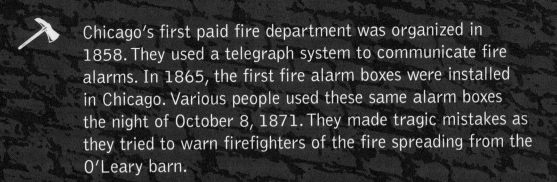

Chicago's first paid fire department was organized in 1858. They used a telegraph system to communicate fire alarms. In 1865, the first fire alarm boxes were installed in Chicago. Various people used these same alarm boxes the night of October 8, 1871. They made tragic mistakes as they tried to warn firefighters of the fire spreading from the O'Leary barn.

How did the fire department make so many mistakes the night of October 8, 1871? Fire alarm boxes were locked to prevent false alarms. No one knows why, but the alarm box at Goll's drugstore never sent the first alarm to the station or to the central fire office. Fire watchers at the courthouse incorrectly guessed the location of the fire in O'Leary's barn. They sounded the wrong alarm box more than once.

Today, Chicago's Fire Department Training Academy sits on the site of the original O'Leary home and barn. Standing at the corner of DeKoven and Jefferson Streets, visitors can view the area where the Great Chicago Fire started in 1871. A point marked on the floor of the academy is said to be the exact spot where the O'Leary barn caught fire.

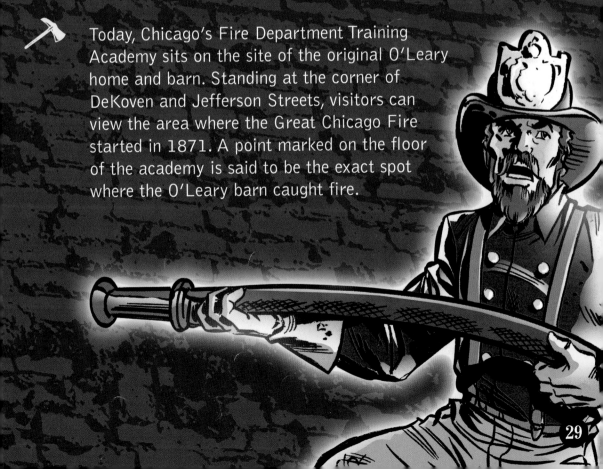

GLOSSARY

fire alarm box (FIRE uh-LARM BOKS)—boxes numbered to show location, placed at different areas throughout the city; a signal from the alarm box sent an alarm to the fire station nearest to the fire.

fire watch office (FIRE WOCH OFF-iss)—a central location in the cupola of the courthouse in 1871 in Chicago; a firewatcher was stationed there at all hours to watch the city for any unreported fires.

tenement (TEH-nuh-muhnt)—a run-down apartment building, especially one that is crowded and in a poor part of a city

waterworks (WAW-tur-wurks)—the system that provides water to a community or town, including reservoirs, pipes, machinery, and buildings

INTERNET SITES

FactHound offers a safe, fun way to find Internet sites related to this book. All of the sites on FactHound have been researched by our staff.

Here's how:

1. *Visit www.facthound.com*
2. Type in this special code **0736854800** for age-appropriate sites. Or enter a search word related to this book for a more general search.
3. Click on the **Fetch It** button.

FactHound will fetch the best sites for you!

READ MORE

Balcavage, Dynise. *The Great Chicago Fire.* Great Disasters, Reforms, and Ramifications. Philadelphia: Chelsea House, 2002.

Cowan, David. *Great Chicago Fires: Historic Blazes that Shaped a City.* Chicago: Lake Claremont Press, 2001.

Dell, Pamela. *Liam's Watch: A Strange Story of the Great Chicago Fire.* Excelsior, Minn.: Tradition, 2003.

Nobleman, Marc Tyler. *The Great Chicago Fire.* We the People. Minneapolis: Compass Point Books, 2006.

BIBLIOGRAPHY

Bales, Richard F. *The Great Chicago Fire and the Myth of Mrs. O'Leary's Cow.* Jefferson, N.C.: McFarland & Company, 2002.

Chicago Historical Society and the Trustees of Northwestern University. *The Great Chicago Fire and the Web of Memory.* http://www.chicagohs.org/fire

Cromie, Robert. *The Great Chicago Fire.* New York: McGraw-Hill, 1958.

Sawislak, Karen. *Smoldering City: Chicagoans and the Great Fire, 1871–1874.* Chicago: University of Chicago Press, 1995.

INDEX